Weight Watchers Smartpoints Cookbook for Instant Pot

The Ultimate Weight Watchers Instant Pot Cookbook: Easy & Delicious Instant Pot Recipes to Help You Lose Weight Fast

Karen Benet

Contents

Introduction

I would like to start off by expressing my utmost gratitude and appreciation to you and your kind gesture for purchasing and downloading my book.

I have tried my very best to make sure that this extremely accessible to Weight Watcher followers of all types (both amateur and experts), in order to help them accomplish their journey with ease.

In doing so, I have divided the book into tiny bite sized portions, each of which are dedicated in explaining a single topic.

This process will help you to easily digest the information seamlessly and help you understand the concept more clearly.

Throughout the whole book, I will be discussing the core concepts of Weight Watchers program while introducing you to some interesting recipes for you to start experimenting on your own!

And since this book is designed to have Instant Pot, I will be including a chapter solely dedicate to Instant Pot as well that is to give you the fundamental idea of an Instant Pot, if you have never used it before.

I welcome you to your harmonious Weight Watcher Journey with your new and shiny Instant Pot!

God Bless!

Chapter 1: Understanding the basics of Weight Watcher

If you just have a peek around the internet right now, you would notice that there are hundreds of different diet plants out there, all of which claim to be the "Very best" and "effective" of them all.

While there are certain diets that actually work and live up to their potential, most of these turn out to be nothing but phonies in the long run.

This might sound a bit harsh, but it is rather true.

Amongst the sea of all of those diets though, Weight Watcher is a diet that has stood the test of time and it now considered as being the 4rth most universally acclaimed diet out there!

Established in 1923 by a humble homemaker named Jean Nidetch from Brooklyn, New York, this diet has a pretty neat origin story to be honest.

If looking from the perspective of Jean, it is safe to say that creating and coming up with the whole concept of the Weight Watchers diet was a very intimate and personal experience for the author.

Why you ask?

Well, Jean was herself an individual who was suffering from obesity and always struggled to control her lust for food and trim down the body fat.

During his journey, she soon had a sort of epiphany when she realize that this is not a problem of her, but rather this is a problem, which is experienced by hundreds if not thousands of people on the planet!

Keeping that in mind, she set out on a quest to explore and experiment with multiple diets in order to find the best one for her and other similar individuals, and in doing so she was able to lose almost 9 Kilos of weight! Which was an amazing feat on its own, however, she was not yet satisfied.

The path to the solution soon made her realize that in the long run, dieting isn't the solution to the obesity problem. In fact, according to her acute judgment, the main source of the problem was "Lack of control"

According to her, it doesn't really matter how good you are at your diet! If you fail to control your lust food once you are out of the diet, then you will gain back those lost pounds.

And this is exactly what she wanted to prevent with her amazing Weight Watchers Diet.

Upon further inspection, she realized that this is a very common problem amongst obese people alike.

In order to help herself and other people alike, she and her friends started support group, which later on came to be known as the "Weight Watchers Organization".

The Weight Watcher's program which is generally followed today is the fruit of all of the hard work that she has done for the program, in order to make it more accessible to a wide range of audiences.

This is a form of diet that does not help you to only trim down your fat, but also improves your physical and psychological health.

So, let's have a look at the basics of the diet now for a moment.

What is the driving principle of the "Weight Watchers" diet?

Unlike most complicated diets out there, A Weight watchers don't really need you to follow a very restricted diet regime when it comes to choosing your meals.

Rather, what this diet does is it slowly encourages people to make healthier food choices in the long run by influencing them to be involved in more physical activities and ingest healthy foods through a very meticulously designed "Point System".

One thing you should know here is that , there is actually a form of Weight Watchers diet that does not follow the aforementioned point system. So don't be confused as we are not going to be focusing on that variation.

The version which we will be focusing on is based on a point system known as the "Smart Points" system.

The recipes that are provided in the book, all work exceptionally well with the point system! However, before jumping into the recipes, let me give you a brief idea of how the system actually works.

In the Points system or Points Plan, specific foods and ingredients are assigned a fixed number of points that are based on the total fat, calorie and dietary fiber content of the meal.

The daily allocated points are assigned to an individual depending on various factors such as sex, height and a few others (including the target weight that is required to be lost).

The only restriction here is that, they are not allowed to eat any food that might exceed their points once the daily limit has been exceeded.

Understanding the mechanism behind the Point System

By now you should know that he point system actually lies at the heart of the Weight Watchers program. It should be noted that the version we are using is known as the "SmartPoints" system, which is an updated version of the previous PlusPoints version.

This unique plan allows an individual to sub-consciously lean towards a more nutritious meal plan.

A simple formula for calculating the Smartpoints of your meal is done using the formula below.

Points = (Calories + (Fat x 4) – (Fiber x 10))/50

However, if you want greater accuracy, then you can always refer to the provided list of the common ingredients (and their SP) in the section below.

As for calculating your daily SmartPoints limit, there are actually a number of amazing calculators out there that will help you to achieve that. Two good examples are

http://www.healthyweightforum.org/eng/calculators/ww-points-allowed/

or

http://www.calculator.net/weight-watchers-points-calculator.html

Just to give you an idea though, if you are male of 20 years and have a weight of 70kgs with height of 5 feet and your target is to lose 10 kg, and then your allocated SP will be 30.

This means that you are allowed to eat as much food as you want as long as you do not cross your daily allocated limit.

It should be kept in mind that the point system does not only include food items. In fact, Smart Points are also allocated to physical activity in the form of FitPoints.

Doing some light exercise alongside your Weight Watchers diet will exponentially increase the effectiveness of the diet.

A list of the most common ingredients and their SP

Below is a list of the most common ingredients alongside their associated Smart Point for your convenience.

Food with 0 SP

- Coffee
- Banana
- Apple
- Strawberries
- Chicken Breast
- Salad
- Blueberries
- Grapes
- Tomatoes
- Watermelon
- Egg White
- Lettuce
- Deli Sliced Turkey Breast
- Baby Carrots
- Orange
- Cucumber
- Broccoli
- Water
- Green Beans
- Pineapple

- Corn On The Cob (medium)
- Cherries
- Cantaloupe
- Spinach
- Fresh Fruit
- Raspberries
- Shrimp
- Asparagus
- Celery
- Cherry Tomatoes
- Carrots
- Yogurt
- Peach
- Sweet Red Potatoes
- Pear
- Salsa
- Tuna
- Diet Coke
- Mushrooms
- Onions
- Black Beans
- Blackberries
- Zucchini
- Grape Tomatoes
- Mixed Berries
- Grapefruit
- Nectarine
- Mango
- Mustard

Food with 1 SP

- Sugar
- Almond Milk
- Egg
- Guacamole
- Half and Half
- Salad Dressing

Food with 2 SP

- Cream
- Avocado
- 1 Slice Of Bread
- Scrambled Egg with milk/ butter
- Luncheon Meat, deli sliced or ham (2 ounce)
- 2 t tablespoon of Hummus

Food with 3 SP

- Milk Skimmed
- 1 tablespoon of Mayonnaise
- Chocolate Chip Cookies
- Sweet potatoes ½ a cup
- 3 ounce of boneless Pork Chop
- 1 ounce of flour Tortilla
- Italian Salad Dressing 2 tablespoon
- 3 slices of cooked Turkey Bacon
- 1 cup of Cottage Cheese
- Ounce of crumbled Feta

Food with 4 SP

- Olive Oil
- American Cheese 1 slice
- Low Fat Milk 1%, 1 Cup
- Cheddar Cheese 1 ounce
- Red Wine 5 ounce
- ¼ cup of Almond
- 5 ounce of White Wine
- Tortilla Chips 1 ounce
- Shredded Cheddar Cheese
- 1 tablespoon of honey
- 102 ounce of English Muffin
- Mashed Potatoes

Food with 5 SP

- Butter
- 3 Slices of Cooked Bacon
- Reduced Fat Milk 1 Cup
- Cooked Oatmeal 1 cup
- Plain Baked Potato, 6 ounce
- Regular Beer, 12 ounce
- 1 cup of cooked regular/ whole wheat pasta
- Hamburger Bun
- Ranch Salad Dressing
- Any type of Bagel (2 ounce)
- 1 cup of Spaghetti

Food With 6+ SP

- White Rice (6)
- Brown Rice (6)

- Peanut Butter 2 tablespoon (6)
- 1 Whole Cup Of Milk (7)
- 20 ounce of French Fries (13)
- 1 cup of cooked Quinoa (6)

Is following the diet costly?

Since the choice of food of this diet largely depends on the individual, it is actually possible to keep the costing of the diet at a very reasonable and low level!

When it come to the ingredients, you will be able to make up your own food plan according to your budget and get the best out of your world!

If you are interested in joining the weight loss community however, those don't cost that much either.

Since this is an organized weight loss program, online membership costs about $17.95 per month alongside a $29.95 initiation fee.

On the other hand, you can also go for In-Person meetings with unlimited access for $39.95 which has its perks as well.

So, for getting the official support from the Weight Watchers community, you may expect a bill of 50-60$.

But then again, that is also depending completely on you!

As for the meals themselves, since there are no dietary restrictions, you are allowed to seamlessly choose the ingredient that fits your budget and create a meal plan that suits your needs and allocated SmartPoints limit.

The only thing to remember is to not cross your daily

allocated Smart Point

Some advantages of the diet

- The Weight Watchers program won't impose horrible food restrictions upon you
- Through the membership and meeting, you will be able to receive various cooking advices and nutritional tips while sharing your own experience
- Even kids are allowed to join the experience!
- The Smart Points system encourages to maintain your portions which will allow you to gradually and steadily lose your weight
- Through FitPoints, exercise is largely encouraged which helps to maintain a nice physique

Some disadvantages of the diet

- Some people might not feel comfortable in sharing their personal information in group meetings
- Keeping track of your SmartPoints all throughout the day might get tedious if you don't have the patience
- Weekly weight loss progress might discourage you as the changes won't be that drastic initially
- The freedom to eat might make it difficult for you to stay in control

And with all of that information, you are pretty much ready to start your Weight Watchers journey!

However, since this book focuses on Weight Watchers recipes using an Instant Pot, let me share a bit of information on the Instant Pot as well just to ensure that everything is covered up nicely.

Chapter 2: Getting the Fundamentals of Instant Pot Noted Down

With the basic concepts of the Instant Pot out of the way, now it's time for you to have a look at the fundamentals of your new shiny device!

So, without rambling around, let's start with the basic question first.

What is this so called "Instant Pot"?

As of recent years, we have seen a number of amazing and very unique devices popping up in the market place that are designed to make the kitchen life a whole lot easier.

Each and every one of these devices are nothing short of a technological revolution! Imagine the Sous Vide device or the Air Fryer!

In short, an Instant Pot is such a versatile device that utilize the power of pressure to cook its meal in no time!

Curious as to know what "Pressure Cooking" means?

Well, in the Layman's Terms, Pressure cooking is the process of cooking a meal inside a sealed up vessel by trapping or otherwise generating steam inside of it.

Instant Pot's works following this principle, but these are much more versatile as you will see shortly.

As for the matter of "How" these cookers are working, well...

Simply put the boiling point of water increases as the pressure increases.

When it comes an Instant Pot, as more and more steam is being generated inside, the pressure eventually increases. This leads to the water reaching very high temperatures without actually boiling up or evaporating which helps the device to greatly minimize the time taken to prepare the meals.

The anatomy of your pot

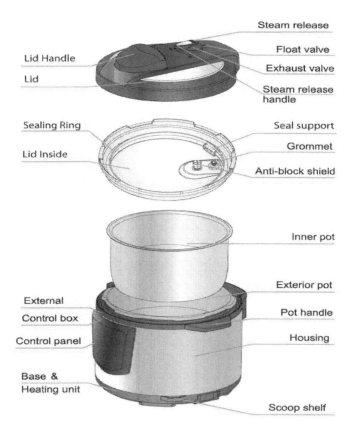

Steam release

Float valve

Lid Handle

Exhaust valve

Lid

Steam release handle

Sealing Ring

Seal support

Grommet

Lid Inside

Anti-block shield

Inner pot

Exterior pot

External
Control box

Pot handle

Control panel

Housing

Base &
Heating unit

Scoop shelf

It should be noted that different companies will try to include something "Special" in order to make their pot unique from the crowd, however the following are pretty much staple for all models of the pot.

- A cooker will have an inner pot which will also be known as a cooking pot
- There will be an electric heating element which acts as the heat source
- There will be sensors that will electronically control the pressure and temperature

The temperature and pressure sensor inside the pot allows the pot to properly maintain and regulate optimal internal temperature and pressure for cooking.

This whole process is known as "Closed Loop Control System"

The process is designed to take advantage of the versatility of the device and make sure that the process of using the pot is as much accessible as possible.

The users are only required to adjust the timer and pressure of the pot, add all the ingredients (following the recipe instructions) and you are good to go!

Instant Pot's even come equipped with a good number of pre-programmed settings that make the process cooking that much more accessible.

The accuracy of these various pre-programmed settings are very high as the settings were chosen after assimilating the data from a huge number of chefs all around the world.

The individual components of a pot

By now you should have a good understanding of fundamentals of the pot, let's have a look at the components now.

Let's go into the details of the individual components now!

The Cooking Pot

The cooking pot is the actual pot where the cooking takes place. Usually the cooking pots are made from Aluminum or Stainless Steel.

If you plan on buying a good quality pot such as the Instant Pot, then make sure to check that the pot has a Stainless Steel pot as they are much easier to clean.

Some pots even tend to have a nice copper plating at the bottom that helps to distribute the heat evenly.

The Locking Mechanism

Instant Pots have something called the "Sealing Ring" or "Gasket" that allows to create a completely air tight chamber inside the pot that allows for pressure build up.

Once the upper lid of the pot comes in contact with the inner pot, this gasket helps to create an internal vacuum that makes the cooking experience much more pleasant and safe.

The Safety Mechanism

Cookers such as Instant Pot tend to deal with a large amount of pressure, so naturally safety is something that is to be taken very seriously.

The good news is that the manufactures of Instant Pot have taken certain steps to ensure that these devices are perfectly safe to use.

The first layer of safety comes from...

Safety Pins: Older models of Pressure cookers had these "Float Valves" that acted as safety pins. Whenever the pressure of the pot would rise, the valves would push themselves up lock itself like a hatch, which would cause the lock to stay firmly locked up.

But these old models actually had a pretty big drawback. They had the tendency of being damaged due to prolonged exposure to high pressure.

The solution to these valves were the updated mechanism that came in the form of "Push Down Pressure Release" System.

Push down Pressure Release: These new and updated valves are protected with innovative "Anti Block Shield" that protects them from wear and tear.

This technique allows the valves to stay intact as long as specified pressure levels are not reached.

Once the pressure exceeds normal levels, the seal position of the valve slowly start to relax it and causes the excess pressure to get released in order to prevent excess build up.

These valves are also controlled by the electronic sensors as well that allows them to help the cooker build up the required amount of pressure and hold it for the specified amount of time.

Positive Feedback Cycle: The mechanism shown below is known as the positive feedback cycle. This makes sure that you are always getting the optimal cooking conditions and prevent hazardous occurrences.

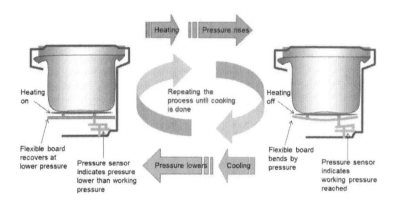

Understanding the buttons of the pot

Some people often think that using a Pot might be extremely difficult because of the number of different options available for the user!

However, that is not the case here. If you have a good understanding of the functions of the buttons, then it's actually pretty easy to use.

- **Sauté:** You should go for this button if you want to simply sauté your vegetables or produces inside your inner pot while keeping the lid opened. It is possible to adjust the level of brownness you desire by pressing the adjust button as well. As a small tip here, you can very easily press the Sauté Button followed by the Adjust Button two times to simmer your food.

- **Keep Warm/Cancel:** Using this button, you will be able to turn your pressure cooker off. Alternatively, you can use the adjust button to keep maintaining a warm temperature ranging from 145 degree Celsius (at normal) to 167 (at more) degree Celsius depending on what you need.

- **Manual:** This is pretty much an all-rounder button which gives a greater level of flexibility to the user. Using this button followed by the + or – buttons, you will be able to set the exact duration of cooking time which you require.

- **Soup:** This mode will set the cooker to a high-pressure mode giving 30 minutes of cooking time (at normal); 40 minutes (at more); 20 minutes (at less)

- **Meat/Stew:** This mode will set the cooker to a high-pressure mode giving 35 minutes of cooking time (at normal); 45 minutes (at more); 20 minutes (at less)

- **Bean/Chili:** This mode will set the cooker to a high-pressure mode giving 30 minutes of cooking time (at normal); 40 minutes (at more); 25 minutes (at less)

- **Poultry:** This mode will set the cooker to a high-pressure mode giving 15 minutes of cooking time (at normal); 30 minutes (at more); 5 minutes (at less)

- **Rice:** This is a fully automated mode which cooks rice on low pressure. It will adjust the timer all by itself depending on the amount of water/rice present inside the inner cooking pot.

- **Multi-Grain:** This mode will set the cooker to a high-pressure mode giving 40 minutes of cooking time (at normal); 45 minutes (at more); 20 minutes (at less)

- **Porridge:** This mode will set the cooker to a high-pressure mode giving 20 minutes of cooking time (at normal); 30 minutes (at more); 15 minutes (at less)

- **Steam:** This will set your pressure cooker to high pressure with 10 minutes cooking time at normal. 15 minutes cook time at more and 3 minutes cook time at less. Keep in mind that it is advised to use this mode with a steamer basket or rack for best results.

- **Slow Cooker:** This button will normally set the cooker at 4-hour mode. However, you change the temperature by keeping it at 190-201 degree

Fahrenheit (at low); 194-205 degree Fahrenheit (at normal); 199-210 degree Fahrenheit (at high);

- **Pressure:** This button allows you to alter between high and low-pressure settings.

- **Yogurt:** This setting should be used when you are in the mood for making yogurt in individual pots or jars

Timer: This button will allow you to either decrease or increase the time by using the timer button and pressing the + or – buttons

The core advantages of the pot

- **Save both energy and time:** Thanks to the added pressure value of the Instant Pot, foods are cooked almost 70% fast in an instant pot when compared to other methods. This process uses much less water while cooking and has a fully insulated exterior pot which minimizes energy loss, allowing even further lowering down of the energy required to boil, steam or cook the meals.
- **Preserve the nutrients of the food while keeping things tasty:** Most traditional cooking methods require you to submerge your produces completely underwater, which greatly wash away the protein and vitamins. In Instant Pot however, very minimal

amount of water is used that prevents this from happening.

- **Kills of harmful Micro-Organism:** Most harmful organism and viruses that cover up raw produces are killed whenever that produces is exposed to boiling pint. In an Instant Pot, since the temperature reaches way above the boiling point thanks to the pressure and steam, 99% of the harmful viruses are killed off. At this level, most if not all of the harmful micro-organisms are killed off. Wheat, rice, beans, and corns carry fungal poisons such as Aflatoxins which might even lead to living cancer. Recent Korean studies have concluded that cooking food under pressure was successfully able to bring down the levels of Aflatoxins to a very satisfactory level.

The simple steps of using the pot

Regardless of what some people might say, using an Instant Pot is actually extremely easy

If you are an absolute beginner in the field of using the pot, then you will find this section to be most helpful!

"How the meals are cooked" and "How the pressure is released"

Now one thing you should keep in mind is that the processes that are used in this book are known as "Water Test"

- Open up the lid of your Instant Pot

- Add a 1 or 2 cups of water into the inner pot of your Instant Pot
- Gently, move the valve to sealing position

- Select your pressure cooker timing, just use the manual button to set it to 5 minutes
- And that's it! Now all you have to do is just wait until the timer runs out! Within 5 minutes, the water should be heated up enough to have produced a good level of pressure

Next comes the process of releasing the pressure.

There are actually two ways through which the pressure can be released.

- **Quick Release:** This method is suitable for ingredients such as vegetables.

- **Natural Release:** This method of releasing the pressure is best suited for ingredients such as meat.

The evolution of the Pot

Since the conception of the device, various features have been constantly added to make the experience using an electric pressure cooker more pleasant. Depending on these features, the devices have been divided in to 3 different generations.

- **Generation 1:** The first generations of the cookers were well known for the inclusion of the mechanical timer and a handful of pressure and temperature sensors. Safety features that monitored the internal condition of the environment of the cooker were also implemented for the first time alongside the basic interlocking lid mechanism.

- **Generation 2:** The 2nd generation of cookers gave birth to the digital control system which not only allowed the time to be controlled, but also pressure as well, thanks to the fact that the pressure sensors were connected to the control panel. Safety features were also overhauled with this iteration as additional sensors were added to check if the lid was closed or not.

- **Generation 3:** The 3rd generation of the cookers is the most unprecedented and advanced cookers out there in the market. These cooker have mastered the accuracy or pressure and temperature control sensors, giving unsurpassable control over cooking. But that's not the only upgrade here! The microprocessors have also been upgraded to the extent that it is now able to perform multiple complex tasks together while cooking. It is easily able to acquire readings from the pressure and temperature sensors and alter the parameters as required. This in turn, allows the device to have pre-programmed cooking settings which helps to make the experience much more pleasant and easy for new comers. All of these, alongside the added safety protection makes this the most advanced cooker to date.

Chapter 3: Breakfast Recipes

A Good morning Egg Roll Bowl

<u>Serves:</u> 12

<u>Prep Time:</u> 5 minutes

<u>Cook Time:</u> 10 minutes

<u>SmartPoints:</u> 1

<u>Ingredients</u>

- 4 cups of cabbage/ Cole slaw mix
- 2 cups of shredded carrots
- 1 can of Bean sprouts drained up and rinsed
- ½ a cup of chicken broth
- 2 teaspoon of sesame oil
- ¼ cup of low sodium soy sauce
- ¼ cup of Teriyaki sauce
- 2 teaspoon of minced garlic
- 1 teaspoon of onion powder
- ½ a teaspoon of ground ginger
- Salt as needed
- Pepper as needed

<u>Direction</u>

1. Take a medium sized bowl and add sesame oil, teriyaki sauce, soy sauce, garlic ginger and onion powder
2. Add broth to the pot
3. Add cabbage, bean sprouts and carrots
4. Cover them with the sauce mix and stir well to combine everything well
5. Lock up the lid and cook for about 7 minutes over HIGH pressure
6. Do a quick release and stir well
7. Season with some pepper and salt
8. Enjoy!

Nutritional Values (Per Serving)

- Calories : 334
- Fat : 14g
- Carbohydrates : 40g
- Protein : 16g

Mashed Up Cauliflower of Magic

<u>Serves:</u> 4

<u>Prep Time:</u> 5 minutes

<u>Cook Time:</u> 5 minutes

<u>SmartPoints:</u> 3

<u>Ingredients</u>

- 1 large sized head of cauliflower
- ½ a cup of low fat sour cream
- Green onions as needed
- Garlic as needed
- Salt as needed
- Pepper as needed
- 2 tablespoon of butter
- 1 cup of water

<u>Direction</u>

1. Add a cup of water to your pot
2. Cut up the cauliflower head, making sure to remove the stem and leaves
3. Put the florets to the pot and top up with water
4. Cook on HIGH pressure for 3 minutes
5. Quick release
6. Allow it to stand for a few minutes

7. Add sour cream, butter and seasoning

8. Take an immersion blender/hand mixer and mash the mix

9. Take an electric mixer and mix the whole mixture on HIGH setting until your desired consistency is reached

10. Allow it to sit for a few minutes more

11. Enjoy with a garnish of onion

Nutritional Values (Per Serving)

- Calories : 213
- Fat : 9g
- Carbohydrates : 2g
- Protein : 26g

The Quickest Pinto Beans from Mexico

<u>Serves:</u> 4

<u>Prep Time:</u> 5 minutes

<u>Cook Time:</u> 30 minutes

<u>SmartPoints:</u> 3

<u>Ingredients</u>

- 1 pound of dried pinto beans
- 1 teaspoon of olive oil
- 1 chopped small yellow onion
- 3 minced garlic clove
- ½ of a medium yellow onion
- 1 can of chopped up green Chilies
- 1 whole piece of jalapeno
- 2 tablespoon of chicken bouillon
- 2 pieces of bay leaves
- 1 teaspoon of kosher salt

<u>For Topping</u>

- 2 medium sized vine tomatoes seeded ,cored and chopped up
- ¼ chopped up red onion
- 2 chopped up scallions
- ¼ cup of minced cilantro

- 3 ounce of mozzarella diced up into ¼ inch
- 8 ounce of sliced avocado
- Lime wedge for serving
- Tortilla for serving

Direction

1. Soak your beans overnight and discard any water
2. Set your pressure to Saute mode and add oil alongside chopped up onion and cook until tender
3. Add garlic alongside ¼ cup of cilantro and cook for 1 minute
4. Add beans, jalapeno, green chilies, bouillon, half onion, bay leaves alongside 6 cups of water
5. Cover the lid and cook for 45 minutes on HIGH pressure
6. Release the pressure naturally over 10 minutes
7. Discard the bay leaves and add jalapeno and half onion
8. Stir in the sautéed onion and season it with some salt
9. Set your pot to Saute mode and cook for 30 minutes until thick
10. Add tomato, scallions, red onion and cilantro to a small bowl and mix them well
11. Ladle the soup into the serving bowls and top up with tomato mix alongside a bit of avocado
12. Serve with tortillas and lime wedges
13. Enjoy!

Nutritional Values (Per Serving)

- Calories : 294
- Fat : 8g

- Carbohydrates : 42g
- Protein : 17g

Tenderly Prepared Apple Oatmeal

<u>Serving:</u> 10

<u>Prep Time:</u> 5 minutes

<u>Cook Time:</u> 10 minutes

<u>SmartPoints:</u> 6

<u>Ingredients</u>

- 2 tablespoon of maple syrup
- 1-1/2 a teaspoon of butter
- ¼ teaspoon of salt
- ½ a teaspoon of ground cinnamon
- 1 cup of dry old fashioned rolled oats
- 1 cup of chopped apples
- ½ a cup of dried cranberries
- ¼ cup of chopped walnuts
- ½ a cup of fat free milk such as almond
- 2 cups of water

<u>Direction</u>

1. Set your pot to Saute mode an grease it up with cooking spray
2. Add oats and cook for about 2 minutes
3. Add maple syrup, salt, cinnamon, walnuts, apple, cranberries to the pot
4. Stir well and add water
5. Lock up the lid and cook for 7 minutes at HIGH pressure

6. *Once done, allow the pressure to release naturally*

7. *Stir in milk and serve!*

8. *Top it up with some other fruits/nuts if you prefer*

9. *Enjoy!*

Nutrition Values (Per Serving)

- Calories: 241
- Fat: 6g
- Carbohydrates: 37g
- Protein: 10g

Sensible Coffee Oatmeal

Serves: 2

Prep Time: 5 minutes

Cook Time: 3 minutes

SmartPoints: 3

Ingredients

For Pot:

- 4 and a ½ cups of water
- 1 and a ½ cups of steel cut oats
- 1 and a ½ cups of pumpkin puree
- 2 teaspoon of cinnamon
- 1 teaspoon of allspice
- 1 teaspoon of vanilla

For Coffee Cake Topping:

- ½ a cup of coconut sugar
- ¼ cup of walnuts
- 1 tablespoon of cinnamon

Direction

1. Open up your lid and add all of the listed ingredients
2. Lock up the lid and cook on HIGH pressure for 3 minutes

3. Take a bowl and add all of topping ingredients and store them in an air tight container

4. Once the oats are ready, allow the pressure to release naturally

5. Serve with coffee topping and milk!

Nutrition Values (Per Serving)

- Calories: 91
- Fat: 2g
- Carbohydrates: 18g
- Protein: 3g

Delightful Sesame and Tofu

<u>Serving:</u> 4

<u>Prep Time:</u> 10 minutes

<u>Cook Time:</u> 7 minutes

<u>SmartPoints:</u> 3

<u>Ingredients</u>

- 2 teaspoon of toasted sesame oil
- 1 medium sized yellow or white onion (slice from top to bottom to about 2 cups equivalent)
- 1 peeled carrot cut up into ½ inch pieces
- 1 cup of peeled and diced sweet potato
- 3 minced cloves of garlic
- 2 tablespoon of sesame seeds
- 1 pound of extra firm tofu cut up into 1 inch cubes
- 1 to 2 tablespoon of tamari
- 1 tablespoon of rice vinegar
- 1/3 cup of vegetable stock
- 2 cups of snow peas cut up in half
- 2 tablespoon of chopped scallions for garnish

<u>Direction</u>

1. Set your pot to Saute mode and add sesame oil
2. Add onion, carrots, sweet potato and Saute for about 2 minutes

3. Add garlic and 1 tablespoon of sesame seeds

4. Saute for 1 minute more

5. Add vinegar, stock and tofu

6. Stir well

7. Lock up the lid and cook for 3 minutes on HIGH pressure

8. Quick the release the pressure

9. Lock up the lid again and cook on LOW pressure for 1 minutes, do a quick release

10. Stir in pepper sauce and a garnish of sesame seeds and chopped up green onions

11. Enjoy!

Nutrition Values (Per Serving)

- Calories: 334
- Fat: 22g
- Carbohydrates: 18g
- Protein: 25g

Magical Stuffed Acorn Squash

Serving: 2

Prep Time: 25 minutes

Cook Time: 30 minutes

SmartPoints: 3

Ingredients

- ¾ cups of dry chickpeas
- ¼ cup of brown rice
- 2 cups of water
- 1 small acorn squash (halved and deseeded)
- 1 teaspoon of oil
- ½ a teaspoon of cumin seeds
- ½ a cup of chopped up red onion
- 4 finely chopped garlic cloves
- ½ an inch of minced garlic chili
- ¼ teaspoon of turmeric
- ½ a teaspoon of Garam masala
- 1/2 a teaspoon of lime juice
- 2 small chopped tomatoes
- ½ a teaspoon of extra lime juice
- 1 cup of chopped up greens such as spinach
- ½ a teaspoon of salt
- ¼ teaspoon of cayenne pepper
- Cilantro, black pepper and paprika for garnish

Direction

1. Soak up the chickpeas overnight and soak the brown rice for about half an hour or more
2. Open up the lid of your pressure cooker and add oil
3. Keep medium heat
4. Add cumin seeds and Saute for about 1 minute until fragrant
5. Add garlic, onion, chili and ginger with a pinch of salt, Cook them for about 5 minutes until the onions are translucent
6. Add spices and mix it well
7. Add lime juice, tomato and greens and cook them for 4-5 minutes until the tomatoes are sauce
8. Add a splash of water if deglaze is needed
9. Add salt, chickpeas, cayenne, rice and 2 cups of water
10. Mix well
11. Add squash depending on the size of your cooker (if possible, add full other add half) to a steamer basket and place it over the chickpea mix
12. Lock up the lid and let it cook at high pressure with the heat on medium-low for about 15-20 minutes
13. Let the pressure release naturally once done and open up the lid
14. Remove the steamer basket
15. Adjust the chickpea rice stew according to your taste (spice and salt levels)
16. Fill up the squash with the chickpea rice mix and garnish with some black pepper and cilantro
17. Serve!

Nutrition Values (Per Serving)

- Calories: 155
- Fat: 9g
- Carbohydrates: 17g
- Protein: 3g

Slightly Manageable Corn on the Cob

<u>Serves:</u> 8

<u>Prep Time:</u> 5 minutes

<u>Cook Time:</u> 11 minutes

<u>SmartPoints:</u> 2

<u>Ingredients</u>

- 8 ears of corn
- 2 cups of water

<u>Direction</u>

1. Husk the corns and cut up the bottom part
2. Wash and rinse them well
3. Add water to the base of your cooker and arrange the corns vertically, making sure that the large part is submerged while the smaller part is facing upward
4. Lock up the lid and let it cook for 2 minutes at high pressure
5. Let the pressure release naturally
6. Serve with some salt and butter

<u>Nutrition Values (Per Serving)</u>

- Calories: 63
- Fat: 1g
- Carbohydrates: 14g

- Protein: 2.4g

A Plate of Mashed Vegetables

Serves: 6

Prep Time: 5 minutes

Cook Time: 10 minutes

SmartPoints: 2

Ingredients

- 2 teaspoon of extra virgin olive oil
- 4 minced cloves of garlic
- 1 cup of diced yellow onion
- 1 cup of diced yellow onion
- 2 cups of diced potatoes
- 1 teaspoon of sea salt
- 1 vegan stuffed roast
- ¾ cup of vegetable broth
- ¼ teaspoon of ground black pepper

Direction

1. Set your pot to Saute mode and add olive oil
2. Add onion and garlic and Saute for 1 minute
3. Add potatoes, salt and carrots and mix well
4. Thaw your vegan roast and add them on top of the vegetables
5. Pour broth on top
6. Cover and allow it to cook for 8 minutes at HIGH pressure
7. Do a quick release

8. Add almond milk, black pepper to the vegetables and mash them well using a masher

9. Slice up your roast and enjoy!

Nutrition Values (Per Serving)

- Calories: 330
- Fat: 13g
- Carbohydrates: 39g
- Protein: 213g

Chapter 4: Soup Recipes

Crazy Tasty Stuffed Pepper Soup

<u>Serves:</u> 4

<u>Prep Time:</u> 5 minutes

<u>Cook Time:</u> 10 minutes

<u>SmartPoints:</u> 3

<u>Ingredients</u>

- 1 pound of extra lean ground turkey
- 1 cup of chopped onion
- 14 ounce can of diced up tomatoes (with roasted garlic and onion)
- 15 ounce can of tomato sauce
- 2 cups of red and green peppers chopped up
- 3 cups of beef broth
- ½ a teaspoon of basil
- 1 and a ½ pack of chili seasoning
- 1 cup of brown cooked rice

<u>Direction</u>

1. Set your pot to Saute mode and add the ground beef (with a bit of oil)
2. Brown it and add onions, pepper, tomato sauce, spices, broth, tomato and give it a stir
3. Lock up the lid and allow them to cook for 10 minutes at HIGH pressure
4. Naturally allow the pressure to release and add the cooked rice
5. Enjoy!

Nutritional Values (Per Serving)

- Calories : 483
- Fat : 28g
- Carbohydrates : 41g
- Protein : 19g

Mushy Asian Soup

<u>Serves:</u> 4

<u>Prep Time:</u> 20 minutes

<u>Cook Time:</u> 25 minutes

<u>SmartPoints:</u> 6

<u>Ingredients</u>

- 2 cups of chicken breast, cubed up into bite sized portion
- 2 teaspoon of coconut oil
- ½ a cup of chopped of onion
- 2 cups of shredded carrots
- 8 ounce of sliced up mushroom
- 6 cups of low sodium chicken broth
- 2 teaspoon of chili garlic sauce
- 2 teaspoon of minced ginger
- 1 tablespoon of low sodium sauce
- 14 ounce of bean sprouts, canned, rinsed and drained
- 2 cups of brown rice
- ¾ cup of green onion sliced up
- ¾ cup of chopped up cilantro

<u>Direction</u>

1. Set your pot to Saute mode and add coconut oil
2. Allow it to get hot and add chicken and onions
3. Cook them for about 3-5 minutes
4. Add mushrooms and carrots and cook for 5 minutes more
5. Add chili garlic sauce, broth, ginger and soy sauce
6. Lock up the lid and cook for about 10 minutes at HIGH pressure
7. Quick release the pressure
8. Add bean sprouts and rice to your pot and stir well
9. Allow it to heat up for a while
10. Serve with some cilantro and green onion
11. Enjoy!

Nutritional Values (Per Serving)

- Calories : 252
- Fat : 4g
- Carbohydrates : 25g
- Protein : 25g

Very Calming Potato and Celery Soup

<u>Serves:</u> 4

<u>Prep Time:</u> 15 minutes

<u>Cook Time:</u> 30 minutes

<u>SmartPoints:</u> 3

<u>Ingredients</u>

- 1 tablespoon of light butter
- 1 tablespoon of olive oil
- 2 large sized leeks
- 1 large sized chopped up onion
- 2 medium sized celery roots
- 1 teaspoon of thyme
- ½ a teaspoon of salt
- ½ at teaspoon of garlic powder
- 1 piece of bay leaf
- 6 cups of fat free low salt chicken broth
- 6 pieces of medium sized celery ribs chopped up
- ½ a cup of fat free half and half
- 1 teaspoon of salt
- 1 teaspoon of pepper
- 1 and a ½ teaspoon of lemon juice
- ¼ teaspoon of cayenne pepper

<u>Direction</u>

1. Set your pot to Saute mode and add butter with oil and allow the butter to melt
2. Add leeks and onion to your pot and allow them to brown up, should take about 5 minutes
3. Stir in potatoes, thyme, celery roots, garlic powder ,bay leaf and salt
4. Add broth
5. Set the pressure to HIGH and cook for 10 minutes
6. Quick release the pressure
7. Open up the lid and add celery stalks
8. Cook on HIGH pressure for 4 minutes and quick release once done
9. Add pepper, salt, lemon juice, cayenne pepper and fat-free half and half
10. Discard the bay leaf and blend the mixture using an immersion blender
11. Puree the soup in your pot
12. Ladle the soup into serving bowls and serve hot!

Nutritional Values(Per Serving)

- Calories : 350
- Fat : 2g
- Carbohydrates : 33g
- Protein : 7g

Rousing Barley and Mushroom Bowl

<u>Serves:</u> 8

<u>Prep Time:</u> 10 minutes

<u>Cook Time:</u> 20 minutes

<u>SmartPoints:</u> 2

<u>Ingredients</u>

- 8 cups of beef stock/broth
- ¾ cup of pearl barley
- 1 pound of baby bella mushrooms sliced up
- 1 piece of diced medium onion
- 2 diced celery stalks
- 2 diced carrots
- 4 chopped up garlic cloves
- 4 sprigs of thyme
- 1 sprig of sage
- 1 teaspoon of salt
- ¼ teaspoon of fresh ground pepper
- ¼ teaspoon of garlic powder

<u>Direction</u>

1. *Add all of the listed ingredients to your Instant Pot and stir well*

2. *Lock up the lid and cook for 20 minutes on HIGH pressure*
3. *Allow the pressure to release naturally over 10 minutes, followed by a quick release*
4. *Remove the lid and give it a nice stir*
5. *Enjoy!*

Nutritional Values (Per Serving)

- Calories : 114
- Fat : 1g
- Carbohydrates : 15g
- Protein : 7g

Coolest Curry Pumpkin Soup

<u>Serves:</u> 4

<u>Prep Time:</u> 5 minutes

<u>Cook Time:</u> 15 minutes

<u>SmartPoints:</u> 4

<u>Ingredients</u>

- 1 piece of chopped onion
- 2 tablespoon of butter
- 3 tablespoon of all-purpose flour
- 2 tablespoon of curry powder
- 4 cups of low sodium vegetable broth
- 1 cup of water
- 4 cups of fresh pumpkin puree
- 1 and a ½ cups of fat free half and half
- 2 tablespoon of soy sauce
- 1 teaspoon of lemon juice
- Just a pinch cayenne pepper
- Salt as needed
- Pepper as needed

<u>Direction</u>

1. *Spray the pot with cooking spray*

2. Set your pot to Saute mode and add onion and cook until they just start to caramelize
3. Add butter with oil and allow the butter to melt
4. Add flour and curry powder and stir until smooth and keep cooking until it begins to bubble
5. Whisk in water and broth, making sure to scrape up the roux on the bottom of the pot
6. Stir in pumpkin, chopped up onion, brown sugar, soy sauce, pepper and salt
7. Cook for 3 minutes at HIGH pressure
8. Quick release the pressure and remove the lid
9. Set your cooker to Saute mode again and stir in fat free half and half
10. Blend the soup using an immersion blender and bring the soup to a boil
11. Turn the heat off and stir in a bit of lemon juice
12. Enjoy!

Nutritional Values (Per Serving)

- Calories : 41
- Fat : 4g
- Carbohydrates : 1g
- Protein : 1g

Delicious Vegetable Noodle Soup

<u>Serves:</u> 4

<u>Prep Time:</u> 10 minutes

<u>Cook Time:</u> 11 minutes

<u>SmartPoints:</u> 4

<u>Ingredients</u>

- 1 finely chopped onion
- 1 large sized diced carrots
- ½ of a diced small sweet potato
- 1 crushed garlic clove
- ½ a cup of frozen sweet corn
- 1 tablespoon of tomato paste
- 1 teaspoon of paprika
- ¼ teaspoon of garlic powder
- ¼ teaspoon of chili powder
- Just a pinch of dried basil, thyme, oregano, parsley
- Salt as needed
- Pepper as needed
- 5 cups of vegetable stock
- 3 and a ½ ounce of uncooked pasta
- 4 handful of spinach
- Spray as needed

<u>Direction</u>

1. *Set your pot to Saute mode and spray with oil*
2. *Add onion, carrots and garlic and fry them for about 2 minutes*
3. *Add sweet potatoes, tomato paste, herbs, spices and give it a nice stir*
4. *Add stock, pasta, sweet corn*
5. *Stir well*
6. *Lock up the lid and cook on HIGH pressure for 8 minutes*
7. *Once done, do a quick release and stir in the spinach*
8. *Season with some salt and pepper*
9. *Enjoy with a garnish of grated parmesan*

Nutritional Values (Per Serving)

- Calories : 171
- Fat : 0.7g
- Carbohydrates : 34g
- Protein : 5g

A Fine Skinny Soup of Steak

<u>Serves:</u> 4

<u>Prep Time:</u> 5 minutes

<u>Cook Time:</u> 20 minutes

<u>SmartPoints:</u> 3

<u>Ingredients</u>

- 1 pound of diced steak, fat trimmed up
- 1 large sized diced onion
- 2 large sized diced carrots
- 2 large sized stalk celery
- 4 pieces of sweet peppers diced up
- 8 ounce of mushrooms
- 2 tablespoon of garlic powder
- 1 tablespoon of salt
- 2 tablespoon of oregano
- 1 tablespoon of thyme
- 1 piece of bay leaf
- 1 cup of crushed tomatoes
- 2 cups of beef stock
- 2 cups of water

<u>Direction</u>

1. Set your pot to Saute mode and add stew meat and brown it up
2. Add onion, pepper, celery, carrots and cook it well until tender
3. Add mushrooms and cook until tender
4. Add salt, spices, water, stock and cover it up
5. Allow it to cook for 15 minutes on the "SOUP" setting
6. Enjoy!

Nutritional Values (Per Serving)

- Calories : 2733
- Fat : 9g
- Carbohydrates : 30g
- Protein : 19g

The Subtle Lentil and Chicken Pot

<u>Serves:</u> 11

<u>Prep Time:</u> 5 minutes

<u>Cook Time:</u> 20 minutes

<u>SmartPoints:</u> 3

<u>Ingredients</u>

- 1 pound of dried lentils
- 12 ounce of boneless and skinless chicken thigh , fat trimmed up
- 7 cups of water
- 1 small sized chopped onion
- 2 chopped scallions
- ¼ cup of chopped of cilantro
- 3 pieces of garlic cloves
- 1 medium sized diced ripe tomato
- 1 teaspoon of garlic powder
- 1 teaspoon of cumin
- ¼ teaspoon of oregano
- ½ teaspoon of paprika
- ½ a teaspoon of kosher salt
- Carrot as needed

<u>Direction</u>

1. Add the listed ingredients to your pot and stir well
2. Cover and cook on SOUP mode for 30 minutes
3. Allow the pressure to release naturally
4. Open up the lid and remove the chicken thigh using tongs and transfer them to a shallow dish
5. Shred the chicken using forks and discard bones
6. Transfer the chicken to the pot
7. Serve with some shredded up parmesan
8. Enjoy!

Nutritional Values (Per Serving)

- Calories : 129
- Fat : 3g
- Carbohydrates : 16g
- Protein : 15g

The Potted Tomato Basil Soup

<u>Serves:</u> 11

<u>Prep Time:</u> 5 minutes

<u>Cook Time:</u> 20 minutes

<u>SmartPoints:</u> 5

<u>Ingredients</u>

- 2 teaspoon of olive oil
- 1 tablespoon of unsalted butter
- 1 cup of diced up celery
- 1 cup of finely chopped carrots
- 1 cup of finely chopped up onions
- 2 tablespoon of all-purpose flour
- 3 and a ½ cups of reduced sodium chicken broth
- 1 and a ¾ cups of low fat milk
- 28 ounce of San Marzano whole plum tomatoes with juice
- 1 sprig of fresh thyme
- ¼ cup of chopped fresh basil
- 2 pieces of bay leaves
- Parmesan cheese rind (optional)
- 1/3 cup of grated Pecorina Romano cheese
- ¾ teaspoon of kosher salt
- Fresh black pepper as needed

Direction

1. Set your pot to Saute mode and add butter and oil
2. When the butter has melted well add carrots, celery and onion and cook it for about 5-6 minutes
3. Add flour and stir well and cook for 1-2 minutes
4. Add milk, broth, juice
5. Add the tomatoes by roughly crushing them up
6. Add basil, thyme, bay leaves and parmesan rind
7. Cover with the lid and cook for 30 minutes on HIGH pressure
8. Give the pot a naturally release and discard the cheese rind and herb
9. Take an immersion blender and blend it until smooth
10. Add /3 cup of grated Pecorino cheese and season with pepper and salt
11. Serve by ladling the soup over your bowls
12. Top it up with basil and 1 teaspoon of parmesan
13. Enjoy!

Nutritional Values (Per Serving)

- Calories : 195
- Fat : 8g
- Carbohydrates : 20g
- Protein : 8g

Heart Throbbing Split Pea Ham Soup

<u>Serves:</u> 4

<u>Prep Time:</u> 5 minutes

<u>Cook Time:</u> 20 minutes

<u>SmartPoints:</u> 1

<u>Ingredients</u>

- 1 pound of green split peas
- 1 teaspoon of olive oil
- 2 large sized peeled and diced carrots
- 1 diced medium onion
- ¼ cup of diced celery
- 2 minced garlic cloves
- Leftover ham bone
- 6 cups of water
- 1 tablespoon of bouillon cube
- 1 piece of bay leaf
- 4 ounce of diced ham
- Chopped up chives

<u>Direction</u>

1. *Rinse the peas under cold water thoroughly*
2. *Add onions,, oil , carrots, garlic and celery to your pressure cooker and Saute for about 4-5 minutes*

3. Add peas, chicken bouillon, water, bay leaf and mix well
4. Cover and cook for 15 minutes on HIGH pressure
5. Allow the pressure to release naturally
6. Take a skillet and place it over medium heat
7. Saute the ham for a while and crumble it
8. Garnish your soup with some chives and ham

Nutritional Values (Per Serving)

- Calories : 182
- Fat : 1.5g
- Carbohydrates : 39g
- Protein : 17g

Chapter 5: Meat Recipes

Benevolent Salsa Chicken

Serves: 6

Prep Time: 10 minutes

Cook Time: 20 minutes

SmartPoints: 3

Ingredients

- 1 tablespoon of olive oil
- 1 tablespoon of minced garlic
- 1 medium sized chopped up onion
- 1 pound of boneless chicken breast
- 15 ounce of sweet corn drained and rinsed
- 15 ounce of black bean cans
- 1 salsa jar of your favorite flavor
- 1 pack of taco seasoning
- 1 pouch of Brown rice

Direction

1. Set your pot to Saute mode and add olive oil, allow it to heat up and add onion and garlic

2. *Stir well until the onion are translucent and the garlic gives out a nice fragrance*
3. *Add the breast over the onion mix and sprinkle taco seasoning on top*
4. *Add salsa, black beans and corn to the pot*
5. *Lock up the lid and cook on HIGH for 10 minutes (manual)*
6. *Quick release the pressure once done*
7. *Take the tender chicken out from the pot and shred it up nicely*
8. *Transfer the shredded chicken back to the pot*
9. *Serve over some rice or by assembling them inside taco shells*

Nutritional Values (Per Serving)

- Calories : 332
- Fat : 10g
- Carbohydrates : 37g
- Protein : 23g

Crazy Balsamic Cranberry Chicken

Serves: 4

Prep Time: 5 minutes

Cook Time: 35 minutes

SmartPoints: 6

Ingredients

- 2 pounds of chicken thigh skinless and boneless
- Salt as needed
- Pepper as needed
- 1 piece of copped up red onion
- ¼ cup of water
- 1 cup of cranberry sauce
- 3 tablespoon of balsamic vinegar
- 1 tablespoon of Worcestershire sauce
- 1 tablespoon of soy sauce
- ½ a tablespoon of garlic powder
- ½ a tablespoon of rosemary
- 1 tablespoon of cornstarch

Direction

1. *Spray your cooker with cooking spray*
2. *Set your pot to Saute mode and allow the oil to heat up*

3. Season the thigh with pepper and salt and add them to the pot, making sure to brown them for about 4-5 minutes (cook in batches if needed)
4. Add chopped up onion to the pot and Saute until they are slightly caramelized
5. Add ¼ cup of the water and work around using your spatula to scrape off the drippings
6. Take a small sized mixing bowl and add cranberry sauce, balsamic vinegar, soy sauce, Worcestershire sauce, rosemary, garlic powder and mix well
7. Mix well and pour the sauce over the chicken thigh and mix well
8. Lock up the lid and cook for 15 minutes on HIGH pressure
9. Quick release the pressure
10. Remove the chicken thigh to your platter
11. If you want to thicken your sauce, then Saute it while adding a mixture of 1 tablespoon of cornstarch and 2 tablespoon of water
12. Saute for 2-3 minutes until thick
13. Serve the thigh with ½ a cup of gravy
14. Serve over noodles or rice
15. Enjoy!

Nutritional Values (Per Serving)

- Calories : 421
- Fat : 7g
- Carbohydrates : 60g
- Protein : 30g

Very Quick "Goulsash"

Serves: 4

Prep Time: 10 minutes

Cook Time: 12 minutes

SmartPoints: 4

Ingredients

- 1 pound of ground turkey
- 1 tablespoon of minced garlic
- 2 and a ½ tablespoon of Italian seasoning
- 1 tablespoon of minced onion
- 1 teaspoon of salt
- 2 pieces of bay leaves
- 1 chopped up zucchini
- 1 cup of chopped red and green bell peppers
- 8 ounce of whole wheat pasta
- 1-14 ounce can of crushed tomatoes
- 1 can of water

Direction

1. Set your pot to Saute mode and add your ground turkey
2. Brown them and add 1 tablespoon of garlic, 2 and a1/2 tablespoon of Italian seasoning, 1 tablespoon of minced onion, 1 teaspoon of salt and finally 2 pieces of bay leaves

3. Toss well and add 1 chopped up zucchini alongside 1 cup of green bell pepper
4. Mix well to allow the vegetables and seasoning to mi everything well
5. Pour 8 ounce of whole wheat pasta to the pot alongside the contents of your crushed tomatoes
6. Fill up the said can with water and pour it over the water
7. Stir well until the pasta is mixed well
8. Lock up the lid and cook on HIGH pressure for 12 minutes
9. Quick release the pressure once done and give it a nice stir
10. Allow the Goulash to cool for a while and enjoy!

Nutritional Values (Per Serving)

- Calories : 283
- Fat : 13g
- Carbohydrates : 13g
- Protein : 30g

Vegetable and Chicken Breast Ala Mode

<u>Serves:</u> 4

<u>Prep Time:</u> 10 minutes

<u>Cook Time:</u> 40 minutes

<u>SmartPoints:</u> 7

<u>Ingredients</u>

- ½ of a Chicken breast
- 2 cups of carrots
- 8 medium sized new potatoes
- 1 cup of pearl onion
- ½ a cup of chicken broth
- 1 spring rosemary
- 1 pieces of spring thyme
- 2 pieces of minced cloves of garlic
- 1 teaspoon of salt
- 1 teaspoon of black pepper

<u>Direction</u>

1. *Season the chicken breast with some pepper and salt*
2. *Spread olive oil on the bottom of your Pot and add the chicken broth*
3. *Stir and add the chicken breast on top of the broth and layer thyme, onion, garlic and rosemary*

4. *Top with potatoes and carrots and season more*
5. *Lock up the lid and cook on MEAT settings for 40 minutes*
6. *Allow the cooker to naturally release the pressure*
7. *Enjoy!*
8. *Alternatively, if you are looking for a crispy chicken, then broil the chicken for 5 minutes and enjoy!*

Nutritional Values (Per Serving)

- Calories : 232
- Fat : 17g
- Carbohydrates : 0g
- Protein : 18g

The Coolest Pepper Steak

<u>Serves:</u> 4

<u>Prep Time:</u> 5 minutes

<u>Cook Time:</u> 20 minutes

<u>SmartPoints:</u> 4

<u>Ingredients</u>

- 1 pound of Boneless Beef Eye of Round Steak
- 80 ounce of sliced mushroom
- 1 piece of sliced up red pepper
- 1 tablespoon of minced garlic
- 1 pack of onion soup mix
- 1 tablespoon of sesame oil
- 1 cup of water

<u>Direction</u>

1. *Add all of the listed ingredients to your pot*
2. *Lock up the lid and cook on HIGH pressure for 20 minutes*
3. *Allow the pressure to release naturally over 10 minutes*
4. *Serve the pepper steak over rice*
5. *Enjoy!*

<u>Nutritional Values (Per Serving)</u>

- Calories : 222
- Fat : 15g
- Carbohydrates : 5g
- Protein : 36g

Generous Taco Chicken

<u>Serves:</u> 12

<u>Prep Time:</u> 15 minutes

<u>Cook Time:</u> 50 minutes

<u>SmartPoints:</u> 4

<u>Ingredients</u>

- 1 medium sized chopped onion
- 1 tablespoon of minced garlic
- 1 pound of boneless chicken breast
- ½ a cup of chicken broth
- 2 tablespoon of diced chipotle chilies
- 1 teaspoon of brown sugar
- ½ a teaspoon of garlic powder
- 1 tablespoon of fresh cilantro chopped up
- ½ of a small lime (juiced)
- Lettuce as needed
- 1 medium sized chopped up tomato
- 12 pieces of 6 inch tortillas
- ½ a cup of shredded cheese
- Olive oil spray for cooking

<u>Direction</u>

1. Spray the bottom of your pot with olive oil and set your pot to Saute mode
2. Allow it to heat up
3. Add onion, garlic and cook them until the onion are translucent and garlic releases a nice fragrance
4. Season the chicken breast with pepper and salt and place them in your Instant Pot
5. Saute until browned up
6. Add chicken stock, brown sugar, chiles, lime juice and cilantro
7. Lock up the lid and cook on HIGH pressure for about 8 minutes
8. Quick release the pressure
9. Shred the chicken and return it back to the pot
10. Scoop ½ a cup of the mix and place it in tortilla
11. Add lettuce, cheese and tomato
12. Enjoy!

Nutritional Values (Per Serving)

- Calories : 148
- Fat : 5g
- Carbohydrates : 13g
- Protein : 10g

Sassy Burrito Bowl

<u>Serves:</u> 12

<u>Prep Time:</u> 10 minutes

<u>Cook Time:</u> 25 minutes

<u>SmartPoints:</u> 3

<u>Ingredients</u>

- 2 pieces of frozen chicken breast
- ½ a cup of uncooked brown rice
- ½ a cup of dry black beans
- 1 -15 ounce can of diced up tomatoes
- 2 tablespoon of minced garlic
- 2 tablespoon of cumin
- 1 tablespoon of onion powder
- 2 tablespoon of chili powder
- 1 and a ½ cups of chicken stock

<u>For Topping</u>

- Romaine Lettuce
- Cheddar Cheese
- Avocado
- Salsa

<u>Direction</u>

1. Add the above listed ingredients to your Instant Pot and lock up the lid
2. Cook for 25 minutes at HIGH pressure
3. Once done, release the pressure naturally over 10 minutes
4. Open up the lid and remove the chicken, shred it up and return it to the pot
5. Prepare your serving bowl by adding lettuce, topping it up with ¼ of the beans, shredded chicken and rice
6. Garnish with some cheese and salt and sprinkle a bit of avocado
7. Enjoy!

Nutritional Values (Per Serving)

- Calories : 309
- Fat : 10g
- Carbohydrates : 46g
- Protein : 10g

Seismic White Bean Chicken Chili

<u>Serves:</u> 6

<u>Prep Time:</u> 5 minutes

<u>Cook Time:</u> 20 minutes

<u>SmartPoints:</u> 5

<u>Ingredients</u>

- 5-6 pieces of chicken breast
- 2 cans of low Sodium Northern Beans
- 32 ounce of low fat chicken broth
- 4 and a ½ ounce of green chopped chili peppers
- 10 ounce can of low fat cream of chicken soup
- 1 can of white hominy
- 1 pack of white bean chili seasoning

<u>Direction</u>

1. Add the chicken breast to your Instant Pot alongside 1 cup of water
2. Allow It to manually cook at HIGH pressure for 15 minutes
3. Allow the pressure the release naturally and drain the water

4. *Shred the chicken using a fork an add chili seasoning, broth, soup, beans, drained hominy, green chilis and a 1 cup of water*
5. *Lock up the lid and cook for 5 minutes more at HIGH pressure*
6. *Quick release the pressure and add corn starch to thicken the dish*
7. *Mix well and serve with a topping of shredded Mexican cheese and hot sauce!*

Nutritional Values (Per Serving)

- Calories : 264
- Fat : 13g
- Carbohydrates : 22g
- Protein : 15g

Mouthwatering Chicken Pasta from Italy

<u>Serves:</u> 12

<u>Prep Time:</u> 10 minutes

<u>Cook Time:</u> 15 minutes

<u>SmartPoints:</u> 8

<u>Ingredients</u>

- 1 pound of boneless skinless cubed chicken breast
- 16 ounce pack of penne pasta
- 2 cups of chicken stock
- 2 diced roma tomatoes
- ½ of a diced red onion
- 1 cup of diced mushrooms
- 2 cloves of minced garlic
- 2 teaspoon of Italian seasoning
- 1 cup of low fat part skim mozzarella cheese
- ½ a cup of fat free cream cheese

<u>Direction</u>

1. Add the listed ingredients to your pot with the exception of the cheese
2. Mix well and add pasta and stir to ensure that the pasta are covered well

3. Lock up the lid and seal, cook on HIGH pressure for 5 minutes
4. Allow the pressure to release naturally over 10 minutes
5. Remo the lid and add cheese
6. Stir well until the cheese has melted
7. Serve with some parsley and parmesan
8. Enjoy!

Nutritional Values(Per Serving)

- Calories : 368
- Fat : 13g
- Carbohydrates : 44g
- Protein : 18g

The Quickest Pinto Beans from Mexico

<u>Serves:</u> 4

<u>Prep Time:</u> 5 minutes

<u>Cook Time:</u> 25 minutes

<u>SmartPoints:</u> 3

<u>Ingredients</u>

- 4 pieces of chicken thigh, bone in and skin removed
- Kosher salt as needed
- Olive oil for spray
- ½ a can of crushed tomatoes
- ½ a cup of diced onion
- ¼ cup of diced red bell pepper
- ½ a cup of diced green bell pepper
- ½ a teaspoon of dried oregano
- 1 piece of bay leaf
- 2 tablespoon of chopped up basil

<u>Direction</u>

1. *Season your chicken with pepper and salt*
2. *Set your pot to Saute mode and spray oil*
3. *Add the chicken and brown it up on both sides*
4. *Spray with a bit more oil and add pepper and onion*
5. *Saute for 5 minutes until a golden texture is seen*

6. Pour tomatoes over the veggies and chicken and ad your oregano
7. Add bay leaf and season with pepper and salt
8. Give a nice stir and cover it up
9. Cook on HIGH pressure for 25 minutes
10. Release the pressure naturally
11. Open up the lid and discard the bay leaf
12. Garnish with some parsley and serve it over pasta
13. Enjoy!

Nutritional Values(Per Serving)

- Calories : 133
- Fat : 3g
- Carbohydrates : 10g
- Protein : 14g

Juicy Mango Chicken with Spices

<u>Serves:</u> 6

<u>Prep Time:</u> 5 minutes

<u>Cook Time:</u> 15 minutes

<u>SmartPoints:</u> 4

<u>Ingredients</u>

- 4 pieces of chicken breast
- 14 ounce of mango chunky salsa
- 1 piece of fresh mango
- Jamaican hot sauce
- Salt as needed

<u>Direction</u>

1. Add 1 cup of water to your pot and season the chicken breast with salt
2. Add the breast on a steamer rack and pour half of the salsa on top of your chicken
3. Place the steamer rack (with the chicken) on top of your cooker and lock up the lid
4. Cook for 15 minutes at HIGH pressure and allow the pressure to release naturally over 10 minutes
5. Remove the chicken, drain it out of the water
6. Add the chicken back to your pot alongside any salsa

7. *Add hot sauce and shred the chicken*
8. *Dice up mango and add them to the pot*
9. *Mix well and serve over rice or with salad!*

Nutritional Values (Per Serving)

- Calories : 720
- Fat : 42g
- Carbohydrates : 16g
- Protein : 66g

Child's Favorite Balsamic Pineapple Pork Chop

<u>Serves:</u> 4

<u>Prep Time:</u> 10 minutes

<u>Cook Time:</u> 25 minutes

<u>SmartPoints:</u> 3

Ingredients

- 6 pieces of thin cut pork chops (bone-in)
- Balsamic glaze as needed
- Seasoning of your choice for the pork chops
- Olive oil as needed
- Cubed up pineapple

Direction

1. Season the chops well (both sides front and back)
2. Set your pot to Saute mode and drizzle virgin olive oil into the bottom of the pot
3. Allow it to heat for a minute
4. Add pork chops to the pot and Saute it well
5. Remove the chop and layer them on a steam rack or trivet
6. Add a bit of glazed on top
7. Add pineapple chunks on top of the chop

8. Add just a cup of water to the pot and place the trivet on top of the pot
9. Lock up the lid and cook for 25 minutes on HIGH pressure
10. Naturally release the pressure and remove the chops
11. Add a bit more glaze and pineapples and enjoy!

Nutritional Values (Per Serving)

- Calories : 621
- Fat : 15g
- Carbohydrates : 101g
- Protein : 24g

Desiring Bolognese

<u>Serves:</u> 10

<u>Prep Time:</u> 5 minutes

<u>Cook Time:</u> 25 minutes

<u>SmartPoints:</u> 3

<u>Ingredients</u>

- 4 ounce of chopped center cut bacon
- 1 tablespoon of unsalted butter
- 1 large sized minced white onion
- 2 minced celery stalks
- ¾ cup of minced carrots
- 2 pound of lean ground beef
- ¼ cup of dry white wine
- 2 cans of crushed tomatoes
- 3 pieces of bay leaves
- ½ a teaspoon of kosher salt
- ½ a cup of half and half
- ¼ cup of chopped up fresh parsley

<u>Direction</u>

1. Set your pot to Saute mode and add the center cut bacon and allow it to cook for about 4- 5 minutes until the fat melts

2. Add onion, butter, carrots, celery and cook for about 6-8 minutes
3. Add meat and season with ¾ teaspoon of pepper and salt
4. Saute for about 4-5 minutes until browned, making sure to break the meat apart using your spatula
5. Add wine and cook for about 3-4 minutes until it is reduced
6. Add crushed tomatoes, ¾ teaspoon of salt and bay leaves
7. Add fresh cracked black pepper
8. Cover and cook on HIGH for 15 minutes
9. Allow the pressure naturally
10. Stir in half and half and garnish with parsley
11. Serve with pasta or zucchini zoodles
12. Enjoy!

Nutritional Values (Per Serving)

- Calories : 126
- Fat : 5g
- Carbohydrates : 7g
- Protein : 12g

Garlic Dredged Cuba Pork

Serves: 10

Serves: 10

Prep Time: 60 minutes

Cook Time: 80 minutes

SmartPoints: 5

Ingredients

- 3 pound of boneless pork shoulder blade roast, fat trimmed and removed
- 6 pieces of garlic cloves
- 2/3 cup of grapefruit juice
- ½ a tablespoon of fresh oregano
- ½ a tablespoon of cumin
- Juice of 1 lime
- 1 tablespoon of kosher salt
- 1 piece of bay leaf
- Lime wedges as needed
- Chopped up cilantro as needed
- Hot sauce as needed
- Tortillas as needed
- Salsa as needed

Direction

1. *Cut up the pork into 4 pieces and add them to a bowl*

2. *Take a small blender and add garlic, lime and grapefruit juice, cumin, oregano, salt and blend well until the mixture smooth*
3. *Pour the marinade over your pork and allow it to sit for 1 hour*
4. *Transfer the mix to your cooker and add bay leaf*
5. *Cover it up and cook at HIGH pressure for 80 minutes*
6. *Allow the pressure to release naturally*
7. *Remove the pork and shred it up*
8. *Return the pork back to the pot and add 1 cup of liquid*
9. *Season with some salt and allow it warm for a while. Serve!*

Nutritional Values (Per Serving)

- Calories : 213
- Fat : 9g
- Carbohydrates : 2g
- Protein : 26g

Very "light"" Cream and Cheese Chicken

<u>Serves:</u> 4

<u>Prep Time:</u> 5 minutes

<u>Cook Time:</u> 15 minutes

<u>SmartPoints:</u> 5

<u>Ingredients</u>

- 7 and a 1/8 ounce of cream of chicken soup
- 5 and a 1/3 ounce of cream cheese
- 2/3 ounce of Italian dressing mix
- 1 and a 1/3 pound of quarter chicken boneless breast

<u>Direction</u>

1. *Add the chicken breast, cream cheese, soup, dressing mix to your pot*
2. *Lock up the lid and Set it to Poultry mode*
3. *Cook for 15 minutes*
4. *Allow the pressure to release naturally over 5 minutes, with a quick release afterwards*
5. *Enjoy!*

<u>Nutritional Values (Per Serving)</u>

- Calories : 231
- Fat : 3g
- Carbohydrates : 9g
- Protein : 41g

Creative Apple BBQ Ribs

Serves: 8

Prep Time: 10 minutes

Cook Time: 35 minutes

SmartPoints: 8

Ingredients

- 4 cups of apple juice
- ½ a cup of apple cider vinegar
- 3 pound of Racks of ribs, fat completely trimmed up
- 1 tablespoon of salt
- ½ a tablespoon of black pepper
- ½ a tablespoon of garlic powder
- Southern Apple Cider BBQ Sauce or the one that you prefer the most!

Direction

1. If your meat piece has the membrane intact, carefully remove it by using a kitchen towel
2. Pour apple juice and cider vinegar to your Pot
3. Set it to Saute mode
4. Season both sides of your ribs with salt, garlic powder and pepper
5. Rub well with your hand

6. Cut up the rib into 2 portions and add them to your pot once the apple mixture starts to steam up
7. Lock up the lid and cook for 30 minutes on
8. Once cooking is complete, allow the pressure to release naturally over 10 minutes
9. Pre-heat your oven to 400 degree Fahrenheit
10. Take a baking pan and carefully cover it using an aluminum foil
11. Transfer the cooker ribs on top of your foil
12. Spread 1 tablespoon of BBQ sauce on either sides of your ribs
13. Cook for about 5 minutes in your oven and serve!

Nutritional Values (Per Serving)

- Calories : 489
- Fat : 14g
- Carbohydrates : 5g
- Protein : 46g

The Instant Barbacoa Beef

<u>Serves:</u> 4

<u>Prep Time:</u> 10 minutes

<u>Cook Time:</u> 65 minutes

<u>SmartPoints:</u> 3

<u>Ingredients</u>

- 5 pieces of garlic cloves
- ½ of a medium onion
- 1 juice of lime juice
- 2-4 tablespoon of lime juice
- 2-4 tablespoon of chipotles dipped in adobo sauce
- 1 tablespoon of ground cumin
- 1 tablespoon of ground cloves
- 1 cup of water
- 3 pound of beef eye of round roast, fat trimmed up
- 2 and a ½ teaspoon of kosher salt
- Black pepper as needed
- 1 teaspoon of oil
- 3 pieces of bay leaves

<u>Direction</u>

1. *Add garlic, lime juice, onion, cumin, chipotle, oregano, cloves and water to your blender*

2. *Puree the mixture until you have a smooth mix*
3. *Trim fat off your meat and cut them up into 3 inch pieces*
4. *Season the meat with 2 teaspoon of black pepper and salt*
5. *Set your pot to Saute mode and add oil, allow it to heat up*
6. *Add the meat and brown them properly for about 5 minutes*
7. *Pour the sauce from the blender to your pot*
8. *Add bay leaves and cook for 65 minutes in HIGH pressure*
9. *Allow the pressure to release naturally*
10. *Transfer the meat to a dish and shred it up using fork*
11. *Return the meat to your pot and season with ½ a teaspoon of salt, 1 and a ½ cups of liquid and ½ a teaspoon of cumin*
12. *Stir and enjoy!*

Nutritional Values (Per Serving)

- Calories : 153
- Fat : 4g
- Carbohydrates : 2g
- Protein : 24g

Mind-bending Chili Verde

<u>Serves:</u> 4

<u>Prep Time:</u> 10 minutes

<u>Cook Time:</u> 15 minutes

<u>SmartPoints:</u> 5

<u>Ingredients</u>

- 3 pound of bone-in Chicken Thighs
- 4-5 quartered tomatillos with husks discarded
- 3 pieces of roughly chopped up poblano peppers, deseeded and stem removed
- 2 Anaheim peppers roughly chopped up, deseeded and stems removed
- 2 Jalapeno chilis roughly chopped up with the stems and seeds discarded
- 1 medium sized onion
- 6 pieces of peeled garlic cloves
- A bunch of cilantro
- 1 tablespoon of Fish Sauce

<u>Direction</u>

1. *Set your pot to Saute mode and all of the listed ingredients and Saute them for about 3 minutes*

2. Lock up the lid and cook on HIGH pressure for about 15 minutes
3. Do a quick release
4. Blend the mixture using an immersion blender
5. Season it accordingly with pepper and salt
6. Add chicken back to your pot and shred it up if needed
7. Enjoy the Verde with some delicious corn Tortillas

Nutritional Values (Per Serving)

- Calories : 332
- Fat : 18g
- Carbohydrates : 29g
- Protein : 15g

Simply Braised Chicken Drumsticks

<u>Serves:</u> 6

<u>Prep Time:</u> 10 minutes

<u>Cook Time:</u> 20 minutes

<u>SmartPoints:</u> 3

<u>Ingredients</u>

- 6 pieces of chicken drumstick
- 1 tablespoon of cider vinegar
- 1 teaspoon of kosher salt
- 1/8 teaspoon of black pepper
- 1 teaspoon of dried oregano
- 1 teaspoon of olive oil
- 1 and a ½ cups of jarred tomatillo sauce
- ¼ cup of chopped up cilantro
- 1 halved and seeded jalapeno

<u>Direction</u>

1. *Season the chicken piece with vinegar, oregano, pepper and salt*
2. *Allow it to marinate for a few hours*
3. *Set your pot to Saute mode and add oil, allow the oil to heat up*
4. *Add chicken and brown for 4 minutes*

5. Add tomatillo salsa, cilantro, jalapeno
6. Cover the lid and cook for 20 minutes on HIGH pressure until the chicken is soft
7. Naturally release the pressure
8. Garnish with a bit of cilantro
9. Serve it over rice

Nutritional Values (Per Serving)

- Calories : 161
- Fat : 5g
- Carbohydrates : 5g
- Protein : 22g

The Pot Spaghetti with Meat Sauce

<u>Serves:</u> 5

<u>Prep Time:</u> 5 minutes

<u>Cook Time:</u> 10 minutes

<u>SmartPoints:</u> 10

Ingredients

- 1 pound of 93 ground turkey
- ¾ teaspoon of kosher salt
- ¼ cup of diced onion
- 1 minced garlic clove
- 1 jar of Tomato Basil Pomodoro Sauce
- 2 cups of water
- 8 ounce of whole wheat
- Grated Parmesan for serving

Direction

1. Set your pot to Saute mode and add turkey alongside salt
2. Stir cook it for 3 minutes, making sure to break it apart as you cook
3. Add garlic ,onion and cook for about 3-4 minutes
4. Add the sauce, spaghetti and water
5. The liquid should cover everything

6. *Cover with the lid and cook for 9 minutes on HIGH pressure*

7. *Do a quick release and serve by topping it up with grated cheese*

Nutritional Values (Per Serving)

- Calories : 390
- Fat : 14g
- Carbohydrates : 44g
- Protein : 23g

Hot and Spicy Picadillo

<u>Serves:</u> 6

<u>Prep Time:</u> 5 minutes

<u>Cook Time:</u> 15 minutes

<u>SmartPoints:</u> 3

<u>Ingredients</u>

- 1 to ½ a pound of 93 lean ground beef
- ½ a large sized chopped up onion
- 2 minced garlic clove
- 1 chopped up tomato
- 1 teaspoon of kosher salt
- ½ of a finely chopped red bell pepper
- 2 tablespoon of cilantro
- 4 ounce of tomato sauce
- 1 teaspoon of ground cumin
- 1-2 pieces of bay leaf
- 2 tablespoon of capers/ green olives

<u>Direction</u>

1. Set your pot to Saute mode and add the meat
2. Season with pepper and salt and brown it up, make sure to break it up using your spatula

3. *Add onion, tomato, garlic, salt, cilantro, pepper and stir for about 1 minute*
4. *Add the capers/ olives alongside 2 tablespoon of brine*
5. *Add bay leaf and cumin*
6. *Add tomato sauce alongside 3 tablespoon of water*
7. *Mix well*
8. *Cover the lid and cook for 15 minutes on HIGH pressure*
9. *Release the pressure naturally and enjoy!*

Nutritional Values (Per Serving)

- Calories : 207
- Fat : 8g
- Carbohydrates : 5g
- Protein : 25g

Tikka Masala Ala Cauliflower and Peas

<u>Serves:</u> 4

<u>Prep Time:</u> 10 minutes

<u>Cook Time:</u> 15 minutes

<u>SmartPoints:</u> 5

<u>Ingredients</u>

- 1 and a ½ pound of skinless and boneless chicken thigh
- 1 and a ½ teaspoon of kosher salt
- ½ a tablespoon of ghee/ coconut oil
- ½ of a chopped up onion
- 3 minced garlic cloves
- 1 teaspoon of grated ginger root
- 1 teaspoon of ground cumin
- ½ a teaspoon of turmeric
- ½ a teaspoon of Garam masala
- ¼ teaspoon of cayenne pepper
- ¼ teaspoon of ground cardamom
- 14 ounce of diced tomatoes, drained up
- ½ a cup of frozen peas
- ½ a cup of full fat canned coconut milk
- ¼ cup of fresh cilantro leaves

<u>Direction</u>

1. Season your chicken with 1 teaspoon of salt
2. Set your pot to Saute mode and add butter, melt it
3. Add onion, ginger,, garlic and 6 spices and Saute the veggies for about 2-3 minutes until you have a nice fragrance
4. Add tomatoes and take an immersion blender, blend well until smooth
5. Add chicken, remaining salt and stir well
6. Cover it up and cook for 15 minutes on HIGH pressure
7. Quick release and add peas and cauliflower
8. Lock up the lid and cook on HIGH pressure for 2 minutes more
9. Quick release the pressure and stir in coconut milk
10. Garnish with a bit of cilantro
11. Enjoy!

Nutritional Values (Per Serving)

- Calories : 226
- Fat : 10g
- Carbohydrates : 9g
- Protein : 25g

Tempting Chicken Marsala

<u>Serving:</u> 6

<u>Prep Time:</u> 5 minutes

<u>Cook Time:</u> 10 minutes

<u>SmartPoints:</u> 4

<u>Ingredients</u>

- 1 tablespoon of olive oil
- 2 tablespoon of chopped shallots
- 2 chopped garlic cloves
- 2 tablespoon of all-purpose flour
- ½ a teaspoon of salt
- ¼ teaspoon of black pepper
- 6 pieces of boneless and skinless chicken breast
- 6 ounce of baby Bella mushrooms sliced up
- ¾ cup of Marsala wine
- 2 teaspoon of cornstarch
- 2 teaspoon of chopped parsley for garnish

<u>Direction</u>

1. *Set your pot to Saute mode and spray it with a bit of olive oil*
2. *Add garlic and shallots and Saute them to 2-3 minutes until fragrant*
3. *Take a bowl and add black pepper, salt and flour*

4. Carefully pound your chicken to an even thickness and dredge it in the flour mix
5. Transfer it to your Pot
6. Scatter mushrooms all around add the Marsala Wine
7. Add ¼ cup of water and lock up the lid
8. Cook on HIGH pressure for 10 minutes
9. Allow the pressure to release naturally over 10 minutes
10. Take a bowl and add cornstarch and 2 teaspoon of water and mix well
11. Set your pot to Saute mode and add the slurry
12. Stir well over Saute mode for about 5-10 minutes until the gravy is thick
13. Stir in parsley and season with a bit of salt and pepper
14. Enjoy!

Nutrition Values (Per Serving)

- Calories: 235
- Fat: 5g
- Carbohydrates: 9g
- Protein: 29g

Close to the Heart Lemon Garlic Chicken

<u>Serving:</u> 6

<u>Prep Time:</u> 10 minutes

<u>Cook Time:</u> 30 minutes

<u>SmartPoints:</u> 2

<u>Ingredients</u>

- 1 -2 pounds of chicken breast
- 1 teaspoon of sea salt
- 1 diced onion
- 1 tablespoon of ghee
- 5 minced garlic cloves
- ½ a cup of organic chicken broth
- 1 teaspoon of dried parsley
- 1 large lemon juice
- 3-4 teaspoon of arrowroot flour

<u>Direction</u>

1. The first step if to turn on your Instant Pot and put it in Saute mode. Toss in the diced onion and cooking fat
2. Let the onion cook for about 5-10 minutes
3. Toss in the remaining ingredients with the exception of the arrowroot flour and close the lid firmly
4. Then, choose the poultry setting and close the valve

5. Let it cook until the timer runs out
6. If you want to thicken the sauce by making a slurry, just remove ¼ cup of sauce form the pot and pour down the arrowroot flour.
7. Then pour down the removed sauce again
8. Keep stirring it and serve

Nutrition Values (Per Serving)

- Calories: 205.3
- Fat: 5.8g
- Carbohydrates: 1.1g
- Protein: 35.1g

Very Fascinating Yum Yum Chicken

Serving: 6

Prep Time: 5 minutes

Cook Time: 18-40 minutes

SmartPoints: 3

Ingredients

- 2 pound of fresh boneless chicken thigh
- 3 tablespoon of homemade ketchup
- 1 and a ½ teaspoon of salt
- 2 teaspoon of garlic powder
- ¼ cup of ghee
- ½ teaspoon of finely ground black pepper
- 3 tablespoon of gluten free organic tamari
- ¼ cup of honey

Direction

1. The first step here is to place all the ingredients in your pot
2. Stir everything evenly to make sure that the chicken are coated
3. Close down the lid and let it cook for about 18 minutes
4. Once done, release the pressure quickly and open up the lid
5. Transfer the chicken and use forks to shred it up
6. Put the Instant Pot in Sauté mode and reduce the remaining juice for 5 minutes

7. *Pour the sauce over the Yum Yum chicken and serve it with vegetable of your preference.*

<u>Nutrition Values (Per Serving)</u>

- Calories: 165
- Fat: 11.1g
- Carbohydrates: 5.1g
- Protein: 13g

Chapter 6: Seafood Recipes

Salmon with Orange Garnish

Serving: 6

Prep Time: 10 minutes

Cooking Time: 15 minutes

SmartPoints: 5

Ingredients

- 4 pieces of salmon fillets
- 1 cup of orange juice
- 2 tablespoon of cornstarch juice
- 1 teaspoon of grated orange peel
- 1 teaspoon of black pepper

Direction

1. Add all of the listed ingredients to your pot
2. Lock up the lid and cook on HIGH pressure for about 12 minutes
3. Allow the pressure to release naturally
4. Open up the lid and serve!

Nutrition Values (Per Serving)

- Calories: 583
- Fat: 20g
- Carbohydrates: 71g
- Protein: 33g

Seafood Paella

<u>Serving:</u> 6

<u>Prep Time:</u> 15 minutes

<u>Cooking Time:</u> 30 minutes

<u>SmartPoints:</u> 5

<u>Ingredients</u>

- 1 pound of jumbo shrimp
- 1 cup of jasmine rice
- 4 tablespoon of butter
- 1 chopped up onion
- 4 cloves of garlic
- 1 chopped up red pepper
- 1 cup of chicken broth
- ½ a cup white wine
- 1 teaspoon of paprika
- 1 teaspoon of turmeric
- ½ a teaspoon of salt
- ¼ teaspoon of black pepper
- A pinch of saffron thread
- ¼ teaspoon of red pepper flakes
- ¼ cup of cilantro

<u>Direction</u>

1. *Set your pot to Saute mode and add butter*

2. *Allow it to melt*
3. *Add onions and cook them until they are tender*
4. *Add garlic and cook for 1 minute*
5. *Add turmeric, paprika, black pepper, saffron threads, red pepper flakes and stir everything well, cook for 1 minute more*
6. *Add red pepper*
7. *Add the rice and stir for about 30 seconds*
8. *Add white wine, chicken broth and mix well*
9. *Add shrimp on top and lock up the lid*
10. *Allow the cooker to cook on HIGH pressure for 5 minutes*
11. *Quick release the pressure once done*
12. *Remove the shrimp and peel it up, return the shrimp to the pot*
13. *Garnish with some cilantro and enjoy!*

Nutrition Values (Per Serving)

- Calories: 318
- Fat: 13g
- Carbohydrates: 47g
- Protein: 26g

Juicy and Melty Shrimp Chowders

<u>Serving:</u> 6

<u>Prep Time:</u> 10 minutes

<u>Cooking Time:</u> 5 minutes

<u>SmartPoints:</u> 8

<u>Ingredients</u>

- 3 large russet potatoes peeled up into ½ inch cubes
- 1 large sized onion chopped up
- 2 medium sized chopped up shallot
- 2 chopped up celery ribs
- 3 strips of lemon zest
- 1 piece of bay leaf
- 3 cups of shrimp stock
- 2 cups of whole milk
- 1 cup of organic heavy cream
- 2 tablespoon of flour
- 2 tablespoon of soft unsalted butter
- 1 and a ½ pound of medium shrimp
- 2 tablespoon of finely chopped fresh basil
- Salt as needed
- Ground black pepper as needed
- White pepper as needed
- Oyster crackers

<u>Direction</u>

1. *Add the potatoes, onion, bell pepper, celery and shallots to your pot*
2. *Add zest and bay leaf*
3. *Add your broth and lock up the lid*
4. *Allow it to cook on HIGH pressure for 30 minutes*
5. *Allow the pressure to release naturally over 10 minutes*
6. *Discard the leaf and zest*
7. *Take a fork and mash up the potatoes using a fork until a chunky texture is achieved*
8. *Pour milk and cream to your pot (setting it to Saute mode) and simmer for 5 minutes*
9. *Add shrimp and basil and give it a nice stir, cook for 2-3 minutes more. Serve it with some oyster crackers!*

Nutrition Values (Per Serving)

- Calories: 590
- Fat: 30g
- Carbohydrates: 30g
- Protein: 51g

Amazing Shrimp and Chicken Risotto

<u>Serving:</u> 4

<u>Prep Time:</u> 10 minutes

<u>Cook Time:</u> 8 minutes

<u>SmartPoints:</u> 5

<u>Ingredients</u>

- 2 pound of shrimp with their tails removed
- 1 cup of instant rice
- 2 cups of vegetable broth
- 1 chopped up onion
- 1 cup of chicken breast cut into fine strips
- ¼ cup of lemon juice
- 1 teaspoon of crushed red pepper
- ¼ cup of parsley
- ¼ cup of fresh dill
- 6 pieces of chopped up garlic cloves
- 1 tablespoon of black pepper
- ½ a cup of parmesan
- 1 cup of mozzarella cheese

<u>Direction</u>

1. Add the listed ingredients to your pot and lock up the lid
2. Cook for about 8 minutes on HIGH pressure
3. Allow the pressure to release naturally over 10 minutes

4. *Open up the lid and stir in mozzarella cheese*
5. *Serve and enjoy!*

Nutrition Values (Per Serving)

- Calories: 463
- Fat: 8g
- Carbohydrates: 63g
- Protein: 29g

Pattern Following English Clam Chowder

Serving: 4

Prep Time: 5 minutes

Cook Time: 13 minutes

SmartPoints: 12

Ingredients:

- 12-24 fresh clams
- 2 cups of Clam juice
- 1 cup of smoked and cured bacon
- 1 medium finely chopped onion
- 1 teaspoon of salt
- ¼ teaspoon of pepper
- ½ a cup of tarry white wine
- 2 medium sized potatoes
- 1 Bay Laurel leaf
- 1 sprig of thyme
- 1 pinch of cayenne pepper
- 1 cup of milk
- 1 cup of cream
- 1 tablespoon of butter
- 1 tablespoon of flour

Direction

1. Add 1 cup of water to the pot and place your steamer basket on top of your pot
2. Clean the shells of your clam and place them to your pot
3. Lock up the lid and allow them to cook for 5 minutes under high pressure
4. Once done, release the pressure naturally and open up the lid
5. Open the clams and discard the clam shells (keep the meat and liquid)
6. The liquid at the bottom of your pan will be the clam juice, keep it as well
7. Wash the cooker properly
8. Set your pot to Saute mode and add bacon
9. Allow it to sizzle and wait until it release fat
10. Add onion, pepper and salt
11. Once the onions are tender add wine
12. Scrape off the bottom of the pan
13. Allow the wine to fully evaporate and add diced up potatoes and clam juice
14. Add thyme, bay leaf and cayenne pepper
15. Lock up the lid and cook for about 5 minutes at high pressure
16. Release the pressure naturally and open up the lid
17. Take a pot and place it over medium-low heat
18. Add equal parts butter and flour and keep stirring it well with a wooden spoon
19. Add this mixture to your pot, alongside clam meat, milk and cream
20. Stir well and allow it to simmer for 5 minutes (in Saute Mode)

21. Serve!

Nutrition Values (Per Serving)

- Calories: 923
- Fat: 25g
- Carbohydrates: 61g
- Protein: 109g

Asian Salmon and Veggies within 15 Minutes

Serving: 4

Prep Time: 5 minutes

Cook Time: 10 minutes

SmartPoints: 6

Ingredients:

For Fish

- 2 medium sized salmon fillets
- 1 clove of finely diced garlic
- ¼ long red chili finely diced
- Sea salt as needed
- Pepper as needed
- 1 teaspoon of honey
- 2 tablespoon of soy sauce

For Veggies

- 200g of mixed green vegetables
- 1 large sized sliced carrot
- 1 diced clove of garlic
- Juice of ½ a lime
- 1 tablespoon of tamari sauce
- 1 tablespoon of olive oil

- ½ a teaspoon of sesame oil

Direction

1. Add 1 cup of water to your pot and place the steamer rack inside
2. Add fillets to a heat proof bowl and sprinkle the fillet with diced garlic, chili and garlic
3. Season with some salt and pepper
4. Take a small bowl and add honey and tamari sauce and pour the mixture over the fillets
5. Set the salmon bowl in your steamer rack and lock up the lid
6. Allow it cook for about 3 minutes under high pressure
7. Cut the vegetables accordingly and place them in a steam basket, season with some salt
8. Once the timer runs out, release the pressure quickly
9. Transfer the steam basket with the veggies on top of your salmon bowl
10. Drizzle the veggies with lime juice, olive oil, tamari sauce, sesame oil and season with a bit of salt and pepper
11. Lock up the lid and set timer to 0 and high pressure, wait for a minute and quick release the pressure
12. Remove the steamer basket with veggies and keep it on the side
13. Remove the bowl the salmon and transfer it to your plate
14. Pour any leftover juice on top and serve with the veggies!

Nutrition Values (Per Serving)

- Calories: 236
- Fat: 15g

- Carbohydrates: 0g
- Protein: 23g

Magical Shrimp Dumplings

<u>Serving:</u> 20

<u>Prep Time:</u> 30 minutes

<u>Cook Time:</u> 10 minutes

<u>SmartPoints:</u> 3

<u>Ingredients</u>

<u>For Shrimp Paste</u>

- ½ a pound of tiger prawns finely chopped up
- 1 teaspoon of corn starch
- ¼ teaspoon of salt
- ¼- ½ teaspoon of oil

<u>For Others</u>

- ¾ stalk of finely chopped green onions
- 2 slices of grated ginger
- 1-2 dried shiitake mushroom
- 20-24 wonton wraps

<u>Direction</u>

1. *Transfer the shrimp to a kitchen towel and dry them*
2. *Chop up the shrimp and add them to a bowl*
3. *Add 1 teaspoon of cornstarch and salt and mix well*
4. *Transfer this paste to your fridge*

5. Chop up ¾ stalk of green onions and 1-2 pieces of shiitake mushroom followed by grating up 2 ginger slices
6. Add the ingredients to the shrimp paste
7. Squeeze to mix everything nicely
8. Take your wonton wrap and scoop up about 3/4-1 tablespoon of mixed paste on one wrapper and gently wrap it up to a shape of your liking
9. Repeat and then place all the Shumai in your steamer rack
10. Pour just a cup of water and close up the lid, let it cook at high pressure for 3 minutes
11. Do a quick release then
12. Serve

Nutrition Values (Per Serving)

- Calories: 204
- Fat: 2g
- Carbohydrates: 37g
- Protein: 9g

The Spicy Chili "Rubbed" Salmon

<u>Serves:</u> 4

<u>Prep Time:</u> 5 minutes

<u>Cook Time:</u> 5 minutes

<u>SmartPoints:</u> 5

<u>Ingredients</u>

- 1 pound of salmon fillet cut up into 4 pieces
- Salt as needed
- Pepper as needed
- 3 tablespoon of brown sugar
- 1 tablespoon of chili powder
- 1 teaspoon of ground cumin
- 1 teaspoon of garlic powder
- 1 diced avocado
- 1 pint of halved cherry tomatoes
- 1 teaspoon of lime juice
- Chopped up cilantro for garnish
- Rice as needed

<u>Direction</u>

1. Add 1 cup of water to your Instant Pot and place the steam rack on top

2. Take a small sized bowl and add brown sugar, ground cumin, chili powder, garlic powder
3. Transfer the fish fillets to the rack and rub them carefully with the prepared mixture
4. Lock up the lid and cook for about 2 minutes on HIGH pressure
5. Do a natural release of the pressure
6. Top them with some avocado and serve!

Nutritional Values (Per Serving)

- Calories : 547
- Fat : 32g
- Carbohydrates : 28g
- Protein : 43g

Chapter 7: Dessert Recipes

Sassy Upside down Apple Pie

<u>Serves:</u> 4

<u>Prep Time:</u> 10 minutes

<u>Cook Time:</u> 7 minutes

<u>SmartPoints:</u> 5

<u>Ingredients</u>

- 6 pieces of Apples
- 2 teaspoon of Ground cinnamon or as needed
- 2 teaspoon of Ground all Spice or as needed
- 1 cup of Graham Cracker
- 4 teaspoon of butter
- Few pieces of caramel

<u>Direction</u>

1. Spray the bottom part of your pot with cooking spray
2. Take a pan and prepare your crust using a cup of graham cracker and 4 teaspoon of butter
3. Pat it well and spread it out evenly
4. Place the pan in your fridge and allow it to chill

5. Slice up 6 apples by hand or peeler and transfer them to a large sized bowl
6. Add spices according to your desired taste
7. Mix well
8. Remove the pan from your fridge and add the apple mix to the pan
9. Add caramel pieces of top
10. Add 1 cup of water to your cooker and place a trivet on top
11. Place the pan in the trivet and lock up the lid
12. Cook for 7 minutes at HIGH pressure
13. Do a quick release and remove the pot

Nutritional Values (Per Serving)

- Calories : 164
- Fat : 1g
- Carbohydrates : 40g
- Protein : 1g

Melt-In-Your-Mouth Rice Pudding

<u>Serves:</u> 4

<u>Prep Time:</u> 5 minutes

<u>Cook Time:</u> 25 minutes

<u>SmartPoints:</u> 3

<u>Ingredients</u>

- 1 cup of rice
- 5 cups of coconut milk
- 1 teaspoon of vanilla extract
- 2 tablespoon of cocoa powder
- 1 cup of coconut sugar
- 1 tablespoon of coconut oil
- 2 whole beaten eggs

<u>Direction</u>

1. Set your pot to Saute mode and add all of the listed ingredients to the pot
2. Keep stirring until the mixture comes to a boil
3. Cover and cook on Rice settings
4. Once done, release the pressure naturally and allow it to sit for 15 minutes
5. Open up the lid and give it a nice stir
6. Top with some raspberry and heavy cream, enjoy!

<u>Nutrition Values (Per Serving)</u>

- Calories: 502
- Fat: 9g
- Carbohydrates: 96g
- Protein: 10g

The Feisty Pumpkin Banana Bread

<u>Serves:</u> 8

<u>Prep Time:</u> 20 minutes

<u>Cook Time:</u> 35 minutes

<u>SmartPoints:</u> 5

Ingredients

- 1 piece of ripe banana
- 2 cups of Pumpkin Puree
- 1/3 cup of water
- 1 yellow Duncan Mine Cake Mix/ Or your preferred one
- Cinnamon as need
- ¼ cup of chocolate chips (optional)

Direction

1. *Take a large sized bowl and add pumpkin puree, sprinkle of cinnamon, banana*
2. *Mix it using your hand and bread up the banana*
3. *Take an electric mixer and beat for 2 minutes*
4. *Add 1/3 cup of water alongside ¼ chocolate chips (if using)*
5. *Add the cake mix and mix everything well*
6. *Take a 8 inch Bundt pan and spray with cooking spray*
7. *Add 1 cup of water to your pot*

8. Add the prepare mixture to the pan and spread it evenly
9. Set a trivet/steamer rack on top of the pot and place the pan in the trivet
10. Lock up the lid and cook on HIGH pressure for about 35 minutes
11. Do a quick release
12. Remove the cake and allow it to cool for 10 minutes before your release the spring form
13. Allow it to cool for 15-20 minutes more and flip it up
14. Gobble up!

Nutritional Values (Per Serving)

- Calories : 243
- Fat : 9g
- Carbohydrates : 34g
- Protein : 6g

Warmly Stuffed Cabbage Rolls

<u>Serves:</u> 4

<u>Prep Time:</u> 10 minutes

<u>Cook Time:</u> 30 minutes

<u>SmartPoints:</u> 9

<u>Ingredients</u>

- 1 small sized cabbage head
- 1 onion
- 1 pound of ground beef
- 2 cups of rice
- 32 ounce of condensed tomato soup
- 8 ounce of diced tomato

<u>Direction</u>

1. Remove the core of your cabbage using a very sharp knife
2. Take a trivet or steamer basket and transfer the whole cabbage head into the trivet
3. Transfer the trivet in your Pot
4. Add a cup of water and steam for 15 minutes on at HIGH pressure
5. Do a quick release of the pressure
6. Remove the cabbage
7. Add rice to your cooker alongside 2 cups of water

8. Cook for 12 minutes at HIGH pressure and quick release
9. Allow it to cool and add chopped up onion, ½ a cup of diced tomatoes and 1 pound of your ground beef
10. Stir well and combine them
11. Once the cabbage is cool, remove the leaves and lay them gently on a flat surface
12. Transfer 1-2 tablespoon of the rice mix into the middle of the cabbage leaf
13. Roll up the cabbage and tuck the sides
14. Add half of your tomato soup can into the instant Pot alongside 1 cup of water
15. Whisk them well
16. Transfer the prepared cabbage rolls to the pot
17. Layer them on top of one another
18. Cook for 15 minutes more at HIGH pressure
19. Quick release the pressure and serve the rolls!
20. Enjoy!

Nutritional Values (Per Serving)

- Calories : 225
- Fat : 7g
- Carbohydrates : 25g
- Protein : 18g

Apple Cheesecake

Serves: 4

Prep Time: 5 minutes

Cook Time: 10 minutes

SmartPoints: 3

Ingredients

- ½ a cup of applesauce
- 4 cups of cream cheese
- 3 pieces of whole egg
- 1 teaspoon of vanilla extract
- Cooking spray

Direction

1. *Grease up the base of your pot with cooking spray*
2. *Add apple sauce, eggs, vanilla extract and cream cheese*
3. *Mix well and lock up the lid*
4. *Allow it to cook for about 10 minutes at HIGH pressure*
5. *Release the pressure naturally over 10 minutes*
6. *Take it the cake out and allow it to cool*
7. *Enjoy!*

Nutrition Values (Per Serving)

- Calories: 690
- Fat: 46g

- Carbohydrates: 63g
- Protein: 11g

A Generous Sugar free Apple Sauce

<u>Serves:</u> 2

<u>Prep Time:</u> 5 minutes

<u>Cook Time:</u> 5 minutes

<u>SmartPoints:</u> 1

<u>Ingredients</u>

- 12 medium sized apple diced and peeled
- Scant ½ cup of water

<u>Direction</u>

1. Start off by placing the apples in the steel pot of the instant pot
2. Pour in the water
3. Cut a circle parchment paper large enough to be able to fit nicely on the pot and cover all over the apples
4. Turn down the lid and set the timer for 10 minutes
5. Once done, let the pressure release naturally
6. Open up the lid and throw down the parchment paper
7. Take a hand-held immersion blender and gently keep blending the mixture until completely smooth
8. Pour down and server

<u>Nutrition Values (Per Serving)</u>

- Calories: 55

- Fat: 0g
- Carbohydrates: 15g
- Protein: 0g

Proud Zucchini Bread

Serves: 4

Prep Time: 5 minutes

Cook Time: 18 minutes

SmartPoints: 6

Ingredients

- 1 cup of melted butter
- 2 cups of brown sugar
- 2 cups of flour
- 2 shredded zucchinis
- 1 cup of applesauce
- 2 eggs
- ½ a cup of heavy cream
- 1 teaspoon of baking powder

Direction

1. *Take a bowl and add all of the listed ingredients*
2. *Take a bread pan and grease it with a bit of oil/cooking spray*
3. *Pour the batter into the pan and cover the pan with a tin foil*
4. *Pour a cup of water into your pot*
5. *Place the bread into the pan and lock up the lid*
6. *Cook for 18 minutes on HIGH pressure*
7. *Release the pressure naturally*

8. *Serve and enjoy!*

Nutrition Values (Per Serving)

- Calories: 270
- Fat: 13g
- Carbohydrates: 33g
- Protein: 7g

Satisfying Brownie Meal

<u>Serves:</u> 4

<u>Prep Time:</u> 5 minutes

<u>Cook Time:</u> 12 minutes

<u>SmartPoints:</u> 6

<u>Ingredients</u>

- 2 tablespoon of coconut oil
- 1 cup of cream cheese
- 2 tablespoon of peanut butter
- 1 and a ½ cup of peanut flour
- ½ a cup cocoa powder
- 3 beaten eggs

<u>Direction</u>

1. Add all of the listed ingredients in a mixing bowl and mix them up using a hand mixer (alternatively you can also use a food processor)
2. Pour the mixture into an oven safe form that will fit your Instant Pot and wrap it up with tin foil
3. Pour two cups of water into your Pot and place the oven safe form inside.
4. Let it cook at high pressure for 12 minutes
5. Once the timer runs out, let the pressure release naturally
6. Serve with some whipped cream or ice cream

Nutrition Values (Per Serving)

- Calories: 700
- Fat: 44g
- Carbohydrates: 73g
- Protein: 15g

Conclusion

I can't express how honored I am to think that you found my book interesting and informative enough to read it all through to the end.

I thank you again for purchasing this book and I hope that you had as much fun reading it as I had writing it.

I bid you farewell and encourage you to move forward and find your true Keto spirit!

Made in the USA
Columbia, SC
10 January 2018